GOLF LEGENDS ALPHABET

Words by Robin Feiner

A is for **A**nnika Sörenstam. This Swedish-American star of the LPGA balanced power and range with pinpoint accuracy. 'Miss 59' was the first woman to shoot a 59 in a pro tournament round, and the first LPGA player to finish the season with a scoring average below 69 (68.70). Legend!

B is for Seve **B**allesteros. The original trick-shot artist, this Spaniard dominated the sport from the mid-1970s to the mid-90s – breaking records both as an individual player and as part of 'The Spanish Armada' when teamed up with countryman José María Olazábal in the Ryder Cup.

**C is for Billy Casper.
Respected for his remarkable
putting skills, 'Buffalo Bill'
was the king of the short
game. One of the most prolific
PGA tour winners from the
1950s to the 70s, Casper
graced the green with his quiet
confidence, unique style
and serious competitiveness.**

D is for **D**ustin Johnson. Along with legends Jack Nicklaus and Tiger Woods, 'DJ' is one of only three players in history to win a tour title in each of his first 12 seasons. His athleticism and powerful swing continue to put him at the top of the PGA Tour.

Ee

E is for **E**rnie Els.
'The Big Easy' has easily
cemented his place as one
of the all-time legends of
the game. The South African
juggernaut won four majors,
earned the title of World No.1
and became the first player to
achieve 300 career top 10s!

F is for Nick **F**aldo.
It's hard to find a more focused golfer than this Englishman. His intense dedication earned him more major championships than any other European player in recent history. He spent a total of 97 weeks as World No.1 and was even knighted for his contribution to the game!

G is for **G**ary Player. Winning a total of 163 tournaments on six continents over seven decades, the 'Black Knight' was named South Africa's Sportsman of the Century, awarded the prestigious Bob Jones Award, and recognized as the eighth greatest golfer of all time. What a legend!

H is for Ben Hogan. 'The Hawk' spent years studying the science of the swing before arriving at a textbook formula. His perfectly poised form was captured in the most iconic golf photo ever taken – with his 1-iron on the 18th fairway at Merion in 1950. The photo and the man, legendary!

I is for Juli Inkster.
Still taking the LPGA circuit
by storm, Inkster is the
only golfer in history to win
two majors in a decade for
three consecutive decades.
Respected by her peers for her
enduring and successful career,
Inkster is a mentor for many
younger players on tour.

J is for Bobby **J**ones. Undeniably golf's greatest amateur player, Jones cemented his place as a golfing legend with his Grand Slam success of 1930. Both athletic and intellectual, Jones was considered the model of the complete golfer – and man. The Bob Jones Award for distinguished sportsmanship is awarded in his honor every year.

K is for Kathy Whitworth. Smashing gender barriers, Kathy won more tournaments (88) than anyone on the LPGA or PGA Tour. She became the top earning female golfer in 1981, was named Female Athlete of the Year twice, and was the Golfer of the Decade between 1968–1977. What a pro!

L is for Lee Trevino.
Practicing with a makeshift
club in his teens, Trevino rose
from poverty to become the
most consistent shot-maker the
game has ever seen – despite
being struck by lightning three
times! Entertaining crowds with
his trademark wit and humor,
there was never a dull moment
with 'Merry Mex.'

M is for Phil Mickelson. With his career producing some breathtaking wins and shattering defeats, it's easy to see why 'Lefty' is such a crowd favorite – the image of the gallery erupting as he leapt for joy after his 2004 Masters win captures one of the game's most memorable Mickelson moments.

Nn

N is for Jack **N**icklaus.
It wasn't just his explosive
shot-making that set 'The
Golden Bear' apart from
the rest, it was also his
psychological edge – he was
a calculating genius on the
course. With his record-making
18 majors, triple career grand
slams and outstanding
sportsmanship, he truly
was the greatest.

O is for Francis **O**uimet. When he beat British legends Vardon and Ray at the 1913 U.S. Open at just 20 years of age, this former caddie proved that golf wasn't just a snooty game for the old and rich. Ouimet became the 'Father of American Golf' and changed the game forever. Legend!

Pp

P is for Arnold **P**almer.
He ushered in the modern era of televised golf, and quickly became its star. Attracting an army of fans with his charismatic personality and humble beginnings, 'The King' won seven majors and 62 PGA Tour titles, and was the first golfer to receive a Presidential Medal of Freedom.

Qq

Q is for Mary, Queen of Scots. This mid-1500s monarch is history's first recorded female golfer. Dressed in her jewels and fancy headdresses, the 'Mother of Golf' would often play a few rounds with her ladies in waiting. It's believed she was also the first to use the term 'caddie.'

Rr

R is for Rory McIlroy. In 2014, 'Rors' joined Nicklaus, Woods and Spieth as one of four players to win three majors by age 25 – putting him on the path to superstardom. The Northern Irishman has spent 95 weeks at World No. 1 and scored a Nike deal rumored to be worth over $200million!

S is for **S**am Snead. Thanks to his self-taught 'perfect swing' – equal parts grace, power and accuracy – 'Slammin' Sam' enjoyed a record-making, 50-year career with 82 PGA Tour championships, over 140 worldwide wins and seven majors. An athlete and a gentleman, he is one of the most beloved golfers of all time.

Tt

T is for **T**iger Woods.
In his prime, he was the
longest ranking World
No. 1 and one of the world's
highest-paid athletes. And
if he surpasses Nicklaus'
18 majors and Snead's 82
PGA Tour wins, he will have
conquered controversy and
injury to make one of golf's
greatest ever comebacks!

U is for Louise **Su**ggs. Pioneering women's golf in the 1940s and 50s, Suggs was one of the founders of the LPGA Tour. Her picture-perfect swing was both powerful and accurate, earning her the nickname 'Miss Sluggs.' Winning 61 LPGA tournaments, including 11 majors, she was a record-setter and fierce competitor.

Vv

V is for Harry Vardon.
While his peers were driving
the ball hard and low, this
trendsetter started hitting
the ball high into the air to
achieve a more controlled
landing – changing the game
forever. The 'Vardon grip'
and the Vardon Trophy are
two lasting legacies of this
legendary shot-making machine.

W is for Tom **W**atson. Fresh-faced but with a killer instinct, 'Huckleberry Dillinger' never gave up. He was a terrific long hitter, but it was his short game that brought the magic. His 'Watson pars'– and rivalry with Nicklaus – produced golf's most dramatic history-making moments!

X is for **Mr. X**, Miller Barber. He had a swing that his peers described as "a man trying to open an umbrella on a windy day!" But the 'Mysterious Mr. X' got his cheeky revenge against greats like Snead and Palmer when he later dominated on the PGA Senior Tour.

Yy

Y is for Byron Nelson.
In his record-setting 1945
season, the gentlemanly
'Lord Byron' won a total of 18
PGA tournaments, 11 of them
in a row. After retirement,
he coached and mentored
another legend, Tom Watson,
and was the first golfer to
have a tournament named in
his honor.

Z is for Babe Didrikson **Z**aharias. Born in 1911, she excelled in just about every sport, even winning an Olympic track and field gold medal, before turning her hand to pro golf. Babe dominated the circuit and later co-founded the LPGA. A female athlete truly ahead of her time – legend!

The ever-expanding legendary library

EXPLORE THESE LEGENDARY ALPHABETS & MORE AT WWW.ALPHABETLEGENDS.COM

GOLF LEGENDS ALPHABET
www.alphabetlegends.com

Published by Alphabet Legends Pty Ltd in 2019
Created by Beck Feiner
Copyright © Alphabet Legends Pty Ltd 2019

9780648506393